Homes on Water

Alan James

Lerner Publications Company
Minneapolis

All words printed in **bold** are explained in the glossary on page 30.

Cover illustration *A floating market in Thailand*

First published in the U.S. in 1989 by Lerner Publications Company.

Copyright © 1988 Wayland (Publishers) Ltd., Hove, East Sussex. First published 1988 by Wayland (Publishers) Ltd.

Library of Congress Cataloging-in-Publication Data

James, Alan, 1943-
   Homes on water/Alan James
     p. cm.
   Bibliography: p.
   Includes index.
   Summary: Describes different types of homes near or on water that people have chosen to live in, for a variety of reasons. Includes houseboats, stilt houses, oil rigs, and lighthouses.
   ISBN 0-8225-2127-X (lib. bdg.)
   1. Dwellings—Juvenile literature.   2. Boat living—Juvenile literature.   3. Offshore structures—Juvenile literature. [1. Dwellings. 2. Boat living. 3. Offshore structures.] I. Title.
TH4890.J36   1989
643'.2—dc19   88-23494
                                 CIP
                                 AC

Printed in Italy by G. Canale & C.S.p. A., Turin
Bound in the United States of America

1 2 3 4 5 6 7 8 9 10 98 97 96 95 94 93 92 91 90 89

Contents

Living on water

Some people may choose to live on water for the pleasure and enjoyment of having a home that is different from the homes of most others. Others live on water because they have nowhere else to live. Some people work on or close to the water, so they make their homes nearby. Throughout history, people have lived on water as a protection from enemies, wild animals, and flooding.

If the land in an area is regularly flooded, it may be safer to build a home on **stilts** where the flood water cannot reach it than on the ground where it might be swept away.

The kind of homes built on water depends on the climate and the building materials that are available. It depends on people's **income**, their needs and patterns of life, and their **culture**.

Homes on water include houses built on stilts, lighthouses, large motorboats, and small houseboats in the harbors of large cities. Some homes on water are luxurious and expensive while others are simple.

Many people live on boats, which come in different shapes and sizes. Rooms on a boat are called **cabins**. The number of cabins varies, depending on the size of the boat. The bedrooms are usually **below deck**. Large motorboats, houseboats, and barges have a **galley**, a bathroom, and often an area used as a living room. Usually, they also have an area to sit and relax outside on the deck.

Above *The sampans in Hong Kong harbor contrast to the high-rise buildings on the mainland.*

Left *These houses in Malaysia are built on stilts to raise them above the flood level.*

Right *This houseboat is on a river in Amsterdam.*

Barges and canal boats

Barges are large, flat-bottomed boats. They carry heavy **cargoes** of coal, iron ore, lumber, and other raw materials to factories along rivers. Manufactured goods are sent by barge to seaports. Some barges have engines and others are pushed or pulled by **tugboats.**

On the Mississippi River, barges travel from Minneapolis through St. Louis to New Orleans and into the Gulf of Mexico. Some journeys by barge take several days. The people who work on the barge or tugboat stay on board at night.

All over the world, engineers have built artificial rivers called **canals**. Ships can travel on the largest canals, such as the Suez Canal in the Middle East and the Panama Canal in Central America. On smaller transportation canals, canal boats are long and narrow, which allows them to pass traffic coming the other way very easily. They can also pass through **locks** without difficulty.

Many canal boats are colorful and attractive. Some people live on them all year long. Other people may rent a canal boat for a weekend or a

Left Long, narrow barges carry manufactured goods to seaports. These barges on the Rhine River carry goods through Germany to the port of Rotterdam, Netherlands.

longer vacation. Canal boats are much smaller than the barges that carry materials, but they have cozy, comfortable living quarters.

In the past, canal boats were pulled by a horse attached to a long rope. The horse towed the boat along by walking ahead of the boat on the **towpath** by the side of the canal. Today, canal boats are driven by engines.

Above The inside of a canal boat has comfortable living quarters for people who spend their vacation on the canals.

Left A colorful canal boat goes through a lock at Guildford, in southeast England.

7

Houseboats

In many parts of the Far East, people live on boats. These floating homes are often tied up close together by the banks of large rivers or in a harbor. People can jump from boat to boat without getting wet. Babies and young children sometimes have a block of wood tied to their backs so they will float if they fall in the water.

Some of the floating homes were sailboats used for fishing. They are now too old to sail, so they are used as houseboats instead. When people go ashore, they walk over a small wooden bridge called a **gangplank** which stretches from the boats to dry land.

Many houseboats in Kashmir in northern India are wooden houses with more than one story built on a wooden **hull**. The people that live in these houseboats use smaller boats to row from their homes to shore.

When boat-dwellers move from one place to another they often take their homes with them. Many work in their boats as well as eat, sleep, relax, play, and raise their families there.

The Bajau people—often called sea gypsies or pirates—live on boats and travel between islands in southeast Asia. The Bajau live on small sailing boats called lipas which are less than 26 feet (8 m) long. A frame of poles, which extends over the sides of the boat, is covered with woven rushes. The boat is kept steady by outriggers, which are long, stabilizing poles at each side.

Right Because of overcrowding in Hong Kong, many people make their homes on boats in the harbor.

8

Left *This elegant wooden houseboat is in Kashmir, India.*

Below *Some Bajau people still live in small boats and travel around the islands of southeast Asia.*

9

Living on a ship

People who work on ships make their homes there. Sailors in the navy, people who work on cargo ships, and the crews of **cruise ships** and other passenger liners all spend their working lives on ships. They often have homes on land, however, where they go for holidays and vacations and where their families live.

There are many different jobs on a ship. Some people help to keep the ship moving. Others look after the crew and passengers—perhaps preparing the meals or cleaning the ship. On cruise ships, passengers may be living aboard ship for several weeks as they cruise to exciting places all over the world. During this time, the ship provides many of the comforts people are used to on dry land. The crew stays very busy.

Of course, people who work on ships do not spend all their time working. Sailors, for example, often stand a **watch** for four hours. Then they have four hours of free time.

The captain is in charge of the ship. Officers help to keep it running smoothly. They check on the passengers to make sure that the passengers are comfortable and that their needs are being met. Both passengers and crew members live in cabins, which are like small bedrooms in a house. There is little extra space on a ship, so it is important for people to keep their cabins neat and use the space they have in the best way.

The cabins usually have bunk beds with drawers underneath for storing clothes. There is a sink, a shower, a bookshelf, and a table and chair. Cabins on the outer side of a ship have **portholes** to let in light.

Left *This navigating officer is on the bridge of a coastal steamer.*

Left *People relax around the swimming pool on the top deck of a cruise ship in the Mediterranean Sea.*

Below *This drawing shows the interior of the* Queen Elizabeth II (QE2), *one of the largest passenger ships.*

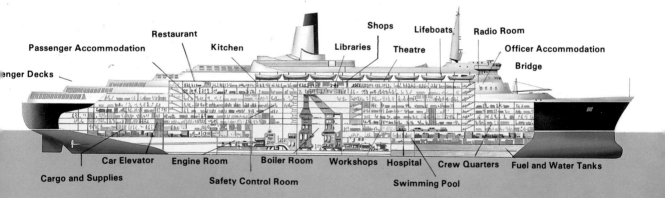

Passenger Accommodation

Restaurant

Kitchen

Shops

Libraries

Theatre

Lifeboats

Radio Room

Officer Accommodation

Bridge

enger Decks

Car Elevator

Engine Room

Boiler Room

Workshops

Hospital

Crew Quarters

Fuel and Water Tanks

Cargo and Supplies

Safety Control Room

Swimming Pool

Floating towns

In some parts of the world, thousands of houseboats make up small floating towns. Boats cover the water in the boat village of Ho Chi Minh City in South Vietnam.

In the port of Hong Kong, many people live on houseboats. Many families cannot afford to buy houses on land and even some who are wealthy prefer to live on boats. Most boats are now powered by motor, but a few are sailboats. The harbor is crowded with boats, which have canvas or wooden roofs to protect people from the sun. Washing is dried over the flat roofs that are even strong enough to walk on.

Above *People fish from sampans in Hong Kong harbor.*

Left *These homes are on the Saigon River in South Vietnam.*

Right *These junks are moored together in the water near Hong Kong.*

People who can afford a big boat buy a junk, a boat with square ends and large square sails. Some junks are taken out to sea on long trips to fish. Others are used for fishing nearer the land.

A sampan—used as a home by poor people—is a much smaller boat, which can be used for catching fish or as a ferryboat to take people across the water. Sampans often have canvas covers to give protection from rain and sun. In most parts of the Far East, sampans have only one mast, but in Hong Kong, some have two.

On a sampan, there is little space for furniture—only some pans to cook with and bedding for people to make themselves comfortable at night. Often the people who help to crew the boat and catch the fish share the living quarters with the family.

Living by the sea

People who live near the sea, such as fishers, sailors, and boat-builders, often live there because they work on or near the water. Other people like to be near the sea because boating is their hobby. Sailing, fishing, or traveling in boats is something that many people like to do in their spare time.

Houses near the sea may be very modern buildings or old cottages.

Many houses near the sea have double-glazing to protect them from heavy storms and strong winds.

Fishing families have different types of boats depending on where they fish and the kinds of fish they catch. A small open boat with an engine may have a crew of two or three people who bait and lay pots in the sea to catch crabs and lobsters. The next day, the same crew goes out to gather the shellfish that were caught in the pots. A small crew might also fish for salmon or other fish using nets. A larger boat may go out to sea for several days to **trawl** for deep-sea fish, with the crew sleeping on board.

Left In the fishing village of Positano, Italy, houses have been built upon steep hills so the people can be near their work.

Right Mevagissey, a fishing village in Cornwall, England, is a popular tourist resort in summer.

In hot places such as the South Sea Islands in the Pacific Ocean, people who live by the sea fish in small boats. In their spare time they relax by swimming or sitting on hot, sandy beaches.

People who live in seaside **resorts** depend a great deal on tourists for their income. Tourists are people who visit the sea on vacations, particularly during the summer months.

Many people run hotels, guesthouses, and camping sites which become the temporary homes of the visitors who have often come from crowded towns inland.

Above An island in the Philippines with cottages on the beach provides an ideal setting for a relaxing vacation.

Rush houses and reed homes

In marshes around the world, green **rushes** grow straight, strong, and very high. After they are dry and brown, rushes can be used as building materials to make thick walls, roofs, and doors. Homes built of rushes are often on an island or next to a lake, near the marshy area where rushes grow. Since rush houses are built with only a door and no windows, they are dark inside.

There are large, wet, marshy places in southern Iraq. The people who live there are called the Ma'dan—the Marsh Arabs. They catch fish to eat, grow rice, and raise water buffaloes. The Ma'dan make their homes using **reeds** that grow in the marshes. Most places are so wet that a building would sink in the water, so the Ma'dan first have to make an island by filling a swamp with mud and rushes.

The Ma'dan cut large reeds, up to 23 feet (7 m) long, and tie them together in bundles. They set the ends of each bundle into holes in the ground so they are secure and curved to make the shape of the house. The houses are large and shaped like a tunnel. The walls and roof are made of mats woven from reeds. In the summer, the walls are rolled back to let cool breezes enter the house, while in the winter, the thick walls keep out the cold wind. Mats cover the floor, making the inside of the house comfortable.

Left *In Peru, people dry rushes and sew them together to make thick walls, roofs, and doors for their houses.*

Above *Bundles of large reeds are shaped and secured to the ground to make the structure of a reed house. The walls and roof are made of matted reeds.*

Right *In this long hall, the Ma'dan of southern Iraq drink coffee, eat, and relax.*

17

Homes on stilts

In parts of western Africa, it rains almost all year round. The land is very wet and swampy and often floods. In these areas, houses are built on long posts that stand in mud. The posts keep the houses well above the water level. Reed roofs are steeply sloped so that rain can run off easily.

Whole villages of houses are built on stilts in Thailand. People visit their neighbors, friends and relatives in small boats. There are also villages built on stilts in Kampuchea, Borneo, and parts of South America.

Houses are built on stilts as protection from flooding. Where flooding is heavy, houses might be destroyed by water and new ones have to be built each year.

In marshy ground in the Netherlands, modern houses are sometimes built using posts made of concrete instead of wooden stilts. Concrete posts provide a very firm base for the house to rest on.

Wooden stilts are made of long tree trunks that have been shaped into a point at one end to make them enter the ground easily. Stilts

Left *This house in Thailand is part of an entire village that is built above the water.*

Right *Some Bajau people now live in houses built on stilts like those in this village in the Philippines.*

and metal posts are often driven deep into the ground by using a heavy hammer. Sometimes concrete posts are made by boring a hole in the ground and filling it with concrete which then sets hard.

Left *This house in Thailand has a very solid structure to prevent it from being destroyed by flooding during the rainy season.*

A city built on stilts

Venice, in Italy, is one of the most unusual cities in the world. It is a city built on water.

Long ago, there were a few marshy islands off the Italian coast. Later, hundreds of thousands of long **larch** poles were pushed through the wet mud of the islands into the clay below. These provided the firm **foundation** on which the city of Venice was built over many centuries. Some houses rise straight up from a canal. People open their doors and step into a boat.

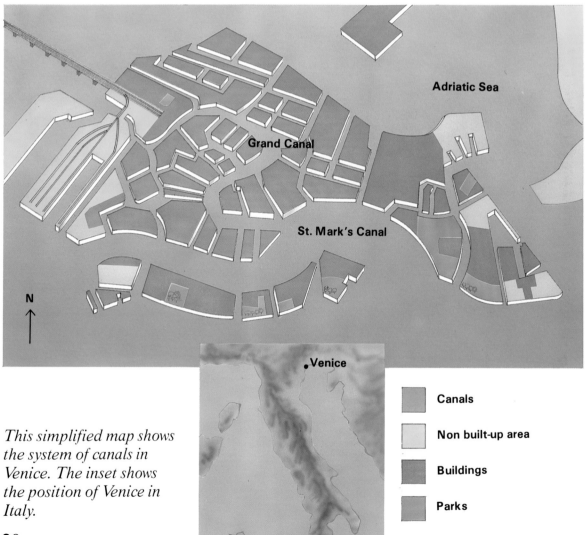

This simplified map shows the system of canals in Venice. The inset shows the position of Venice in Italy.

Grand Canal

Adriatic Sea

St. Mark's Canal

N

Venice

■ Canals

□ Non built-up area

■ Buildings

■ Parks

Today, Venice consists of about 120 islands. These islands are joined by about 400 bridges. There are no cars or other road vehicles because most of the streets are canals of water, where boats of all kinds—including the famous gondolas—travel as taxis, delivery boats, and tourist boats. The rest of the streets are for pedestrians. There is as much traffic on the walking streets and canals as there is on the streets of any usual town.

In the past, people found that when strong winds blew from the sea toward the city, the water level would rise up the side of buildings and flood rooms on the ground floor. Squares and other walking places were also flooded. But now huge **barriers** have been built which can be raised to stop the sea from flooding most of Venice. Today, attempts are being made to stop the city from sinking.

A raised **causeway** about two and a half miles (4 km) long joins the islands of Venice with the rest of Italy. People cross this causeway to Venice in trains and other vehicles, but once they have arrived in the city, they must walk or take a boat.

Above *The Grand Canal in Venice*

Below *Several gondolas carry people along a narrow canal in Venice.*

21

An oil rig

A drilling rig is a huge platform that is towed out to sea by a ship to search for oil. There is a drilling pipe that goes down into the rock under the sea. Once oil has been found, the drilling rig is taken away.

A second rig, called a production rig, is brought to pump oil from under the ground. The oil is pumped through a pipeline under the sea to a **refinery** on land.

Inside an oil rig, there are rooms where many people work and places where they can relax when they are not working. There are bedrooms, **recreation** rooms, dining rooms, and shower rooms.

An oil rig is like a small town. People do not leave the oil rig when they have finished work for the day. They must stay there until they get "shore leave" for a few weeks. When one crew gets a leave, a helicopter brings in a replacement crew and takes the original crew away. When they are needed, supply boats bring drinking water and food for the crew.

Left An oil rig is towed out to sea by a tugboat.

Right There seems to be nothing unusual about this cafeteria, even though it is on an oil rig in the North Sea.

Above A helicopter lands on an oil rig in Mexico carrying a replacement crew.

Left This oil rig is off the coast of Finland.

On the rig, there is a radio room where messages are relayed. It is important for people working on an oil rig to know accurate weather forecasts so they are well prepared for storms and **gale force** winds.

Different shifts of workers keep the oil rig pumping around the clock. At any one time an oil rig has 60 to 80 people living on it.

Lighthouses and lightships

Wherever ships travel, there are natural dangers. These include sharp rocks close to the surface of the water, strong currents, sandbanks, and icebergs. Lighthouses are built at the end of a piece of land or on a large rock out at sea that is near a danger. The light from lighthouses warns passing ships from coming too close.

At the top of a lighthouse is a lantern—a huge warning light that slowly rotates. When sailors see this light, they are warned to keep away from that area or to contact the lighthouse by radio to find out what danger their ship is facing.

A rock lighthouse is a tower built of large blocks on a solid base. Most lighthouses are circular towers with many floors that are reached by a **spiral** staircase. There are bedrooms, a living room, bathroom, and kitchen, as well as a room at the top near the lantern where the lighthouse keeper watches for passing ships. In round lighthouses, the furniture is curved to fit snugly against the walls. Even the beds are made with a curve.

The keepers work in shifts of two months in the lighthouse and

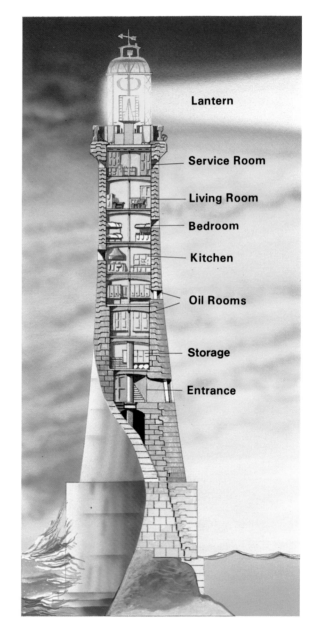

Lantern

Service Room

Living Room

Bedroom

Kitchen

Oil Rooms

Storage

Entrance

Above This drawing shows a cross section of a lighthouse with the rooms inside.

24

one month away. The number of lighthouse keepers depends on the size of the lighthouse. The keepers are taken to the lighthouse by boat or helicopter. When they land at the base, they climb up iron rungs on the side of the building to reach the door. Some lighthouses that work **automatically** do not need keepers at all.

A lightship is an anchored boat that, like a lighthouse, has a large light that rotates and radio contact with passing ships. Each lightship has a working crew of about eight people who live on the ship.

Above This lighthouse on the coast of Maine was built to warn passing ships of dangerous hidden rocks.

Right Lightships are positioned in places where lighthouses cannot be built. This lightship is moored off the coast of Australia.

Living under the sea

The farther down one travels beneath the surface of the water, the greater the pressure of the water and the less the sunlight can penetrate. It may seem strange, but people can make their homes and live under the water. Scientists have built special vehicles in which people have lived deep under water for quite long periods of time.

One vehicle, called Starfish House because it has parts (or arms) shaped like a starfish, was anchored to the bed of the Red Sea. A group of men lived in Starfish House for four weeks as a scientific experiment.

They left their underwater home each day wearing diving suits and carrying oxygen cylinders to allow them to breathe underwater. They caught and studied fish and collected underwater plants. Air for their steel home—33 feet (10 m) under the surface of the water—was pumped down to the house from the surface of the water.

Starfish House was comfortable inside, with bunks for sleeping, a kitchen, a bathroom, and a living room. The men could go swimming outside—though they had to keep a lookout for sharks.

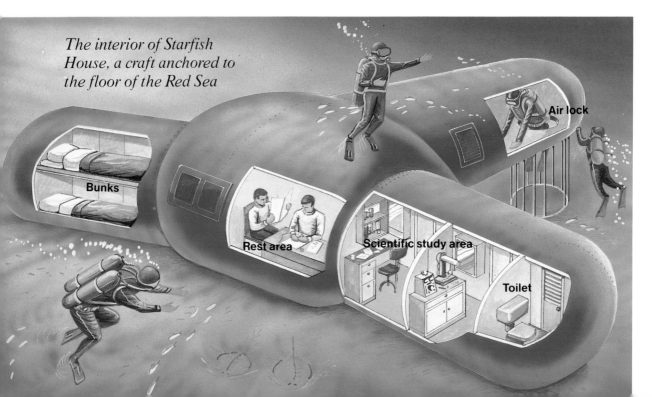

The interior of Starfish House, a craft anchored to the floor of the Red Sea

Bunks

Air lock

Rest area

Scientific study area

Toilet

Left This is Hotel Atlantis, a model of an underwater craft designed for the future.

Below The crew of the submarine USS Ohio has to adapt to living for long periods of time in their home under the sea.

Submarines are ships that can travel on the surface of the sea or deep under the waves. The crew must get accustomed to living a strange life traveling in the sea. Submarines have cabins, just like an ordinary ship, but conditions are cramped. The crew might not see daylight for months.

In the future, it will probably be possible to go on vacation under the sea and stay in an underwater hotel.

Homes near rivers and lakes

Many people live close to rivers and lakes because they find pleasure in hobbies such as boating, fishing, and swimming.

Boating is a favorite hobby for many people. Many children learn how to paddle a small rubber **inflatable** boat. When they are older they may learn how to handle the oars of a small wooden rowing boat. Later, they may learn how to sail a small **dinghy.**

Some people own canoes, sailboats, or motorboats. People with homes very close to rivers or lakes may have their own dock and a boathouse where they keep their boats at night.

Above A family enjoys a trip on a small rowboat.

Left The crew skillfully handles a boat in the turbulent waters of the River Ottawa in Canada.

28

There are many lakes in countries all over the world where people enjoy boating for recreation. These countries include the United States, Great Britain, Canada, and Finland. Many families in these countries have small vacation homes by the sea, on the shores of a lake, or on the banks of a river.

People with homes near rivers and lakes often take great pleasure swimming there if the water is clean and fresh.

Many villagers living on the banks of the River Mekong in Thailand swim in the river each day before their evening meal. This cools and relaxes them in their hot climate.

Vacationers make their temporary homes in tents, resorts, or housekeeping cottages to be near lakes or rivers which are set in beautiful countryside.

Water interests and fascinates many people. People who live in villages along the coast say that the sea is "in their blood" and they would not be happy living anywhere else.

Left Many people who enjoy the water have vacation homes on the shores of lakes like this in one in Finland.

Glossary

automatic Working without human help

barriers Gates to prevent something from passing through

below deck Under the deck of a ship or smaller boat

cabins Rooms on a boat or bedrooms on a ship

canal An artificial water channel

cargo The goods carried by ship

causeway A raised road over water

cruise ship A ship that vacationers travel on for pleasure

culture The way of life shared by a group of people, including their language, arts, and beliefs

dinghy A small boat with oars and sometimes sails

foundation The base on which the walls of a building stand

gale force Very strong wind, traveling between 32 and 63 miles per hour (51-101 km/h)

galley A small kitchen

gangplank A wooden plank that acts as a bridge between one boat and another boat or the shore

hull The frame and the body of a ship

income The amount of money a person or family earns

inflatable A boat with air inside its hull to keep it afloat

larch A tree with very tough, strong wood

locks A part of a canal that can be closed off by gates. The water level can be raised or lowered to allow boats to pass from one level of water to another.

porthole A small, circular window in the side of a boat

recreation A hobby or pastime for enjoyment or relaxation

reeds Tall marsh plants with firm stems

refinery A place where crude oil is purified

resort A place where people go on vacation

rushes Waterside plants with stems that are wider at the bottom and thinner at the top

spiral A coiled shape that winds around a central point

stilts Wooden poles firmly driven into the ground to support a building above them

towpath A path running parallel to a canal from which an animal helped tow a canal boat

tugboat A small boat used to pull or push a barge or a larger boat

trawl Fishing with a large net shaped like a bag with its wide mouth held open. It is dragged along the bottom of the sea to collect fish.

watch A period of time spent on duty, perhaps at a look-out post

Books to read

River and Canal by Edward Boyer (Holiday House, 1986)
The Barge Book by Jerry Bushey (Carolrhoda Books, 1984)
On the Waterway by Malcolm Dixon (The Bookwright Press, 1984)
Submarines by Tony Gibbons (Lerner Publications, 1987)
Canals by Cass R. Sandak (Franklin Watts, 1983)
Life on a Barge by Huck Scarry (Prentice-Hall, 1982)

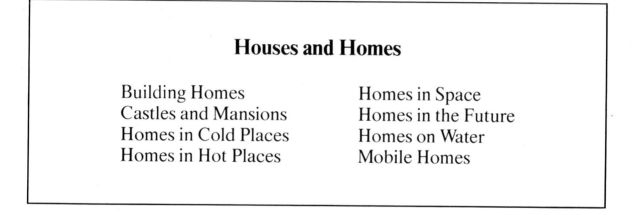

Houses and Homes

Building Homes	Homes in Space
Castles and Mansions	Homes in the Future
Homes in Cold Places	Homes on Water
Homes in Hot Places	Mobile Homes

Picture acknowledgements

The author and publishers would like to thank the following for the illustrations in this book: British Waterways Board, p.7 (top); Chapel Studios, p.21 (bottom); The Hutchison Library, pp.9 (top), 13, 16, 17, 21 (top), 23 (top right and left); Christine Osborne, pp.4, 11; Photri, p.27; Topham, pp.6, 9 (bottom), 10, 23 (bottom), 25 (bottom), 29; ZEFA, pp.5 (bottom), 7 (bottom), 8, 12, 14, 15, 18, 19, 22, 25 (top), 28 (top). All other pictures from the Wayland Picture Library. Christine Osborne, *cover.*

31

Index